1

Grammar through text types

PETER **DURKIN**
HEATHER **SPERRING**
VIRGINIA **FERGUSON**

OXFORD
UNIVERSITY PRESS
AUSTRALIA & NEW ZEALAND

OXFORD
UNIVERSITY PRESS

Oxford University Press is a department of the University of Oxford. It furthers the University's objective of excellence in research, scholarship, and education by publishing worldwide. Oxford is a registered trademark of Oxford University Press in the UK and in certain other countries.

Published in Australia by
Oxford University Press
Level 8, 737 Bourke Street, Docklands, Victoria 3008, Australia

First published 2008
Reprinted 2009, 2010, 2011, 2012, 2013, 2014, 2016 (twice), 2017, 2018, 2019, 2020, 2021, 2023, 2024

ISBN 978 0 19 556036 7

Typeset Alice Graphics
Illustrated by Rob Mancini
Printed in India by Manipal Technologies Limited

Acknowledgements

The author and publisher wish to thank the following copyright holders for granting permission to reproduce their material.

Fisher, Aileen c/o Marian Reiner Literacy Agent, 'My Puppy', p. 44 © Aileen Fisher.

Every effort has been made to trace the original source of copyright material contained in this book. The publisher would be pleased to hear from copyright holders to rectify any errors or omissions.

Contents

Introduction

Grammar Through Text Types uses factual and literary texts as the context for introducing basic grammar skills to primary school students:

Recount	Description	Exposition
Narrative	Explanation	Information Report
Poetry	Procedure	Transaction

The comprehensive range of grammatical conventions covered meets the requirements as outlined in the state and territory standards for primary schools.

The series consists of:

- Six workbooks with 30 double-page units covering a year's work at the relevant level
- A simple answer section located at the centre of the books
- Revision units that review important grammatical conventions at word, sentence and text level.

How to use this book

The *left-hand page* of each unit focuses on a particular grammatical convention within a specific text type. The text sample for each unit has been chosen to provide:

- examples in context of the particular grammatical convention that is the focus of that unit
- a model of a particular text type that the students can then use as a basis for their own writing.

Left-hand page

Grammar focus

The left-hand column is used to highlight, in context, the particular grammatical feature.

Activities related to the grammatical feature

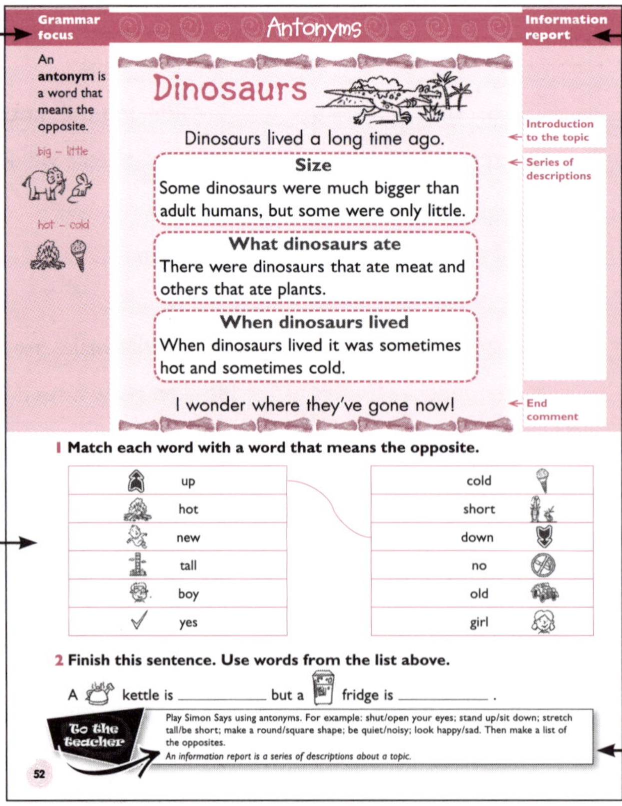
Grammar focus
Antonyms
Information report
An **antonym** is a word that means the opposite.
big – little
hot – cold
Dinosaurs
Dinosaurs lived a long time ago.
Introduction to the topic
Series of descriptions
Size
Some dinosaurs were much bigger than adult humans, but some were only little.
What dinosaurs ate
There were dinosaurs that ate meat and others that ate plants.
When dinosaurs lived
When dinosaurs lived it was sometimes hot and sometimes cold.
I wonder where they've gone now!
End comment

1 Match each word with a word that means the opposite.

up	cold
hot	short
new	down
tall	no
boy	old
yes	girl

2 Finish this sentence. Use words from the list above.

A kettle is ________ but a fridge is ________ .

To the teacher

Play Simon Says using antonyms. For example: shut/open your eyes; stand up/sit down; stretch tall/be short; make a round/square shape; be quiet/noisy; look happy/sad. Then make a list of the opposites.

An information report is a series of descriptions about a topic.

52

Text type

The right-hand column is used to highlight the various features and structure of a particular text type.

A model for writing

A language model grounded in the relationship between text type and grammar

To the teacher

Advice and directions related to both the grammar and the text type

These are nouns:

pencil 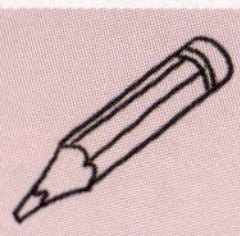

mountain 

butterfly 

bike 

3 Write the noun from the Word bank to match these pictures below.

h __ __

a __ __ l e

e __ __

c __ __

s __ __ __ s

p __ __

Noun Word bank

pig
car
apple
hat
socks
egg

4 Write a noun to match each sentence, and then draw each noun.

I like to ride it.

b ________

I like to wear it.

____

I am a pet.

____

Your turn to write

Draw a picture of a time you hurt yourself. Write a sentence about it and draw a circle around the nouns you use.

Common nouns

Nouns
Nouns are naming words.

pizza 

cheese 

pineapple 

meat 

I love pizza

Pizza
Yellow cheese
Juicy pineapple
Tasty meat
Yummy pizza
I love pizza!
by Holli

← **Title** What I like most

← **My opinion** Why I like pizza

← **Ending** What I think

← **Author**

1 Read the poem and write down the nouns that match these pictures.

a  c ___ ___ ___ s e

b  m e a ___

c  p ___ ___ ___ a

d  p ___ ___ ___ a p p l e

2 Draw and/or write two more things you like to have on a pizza:

To the teacher

Play a memory game. Start with, "I am having pizza for tea. On it will be . . ." As each child has a turn they must remember and say what other children have said, and then add their own suggestions – and they could be silly ones, for example, ice-cream, bananas, toothpaste, chocolate and so on. Tell children that these words are all nouns.

An exposition is when you say what you think and feel about a topic (point of view).

These are nouns.

hat  dog  girl  cake 

3 Write the nouns to match the pictures. Use the Word bank to help you.

Word bank

egg  eye  bag  bowl 

hand  T-shirt  ear  hair 

4 Draw three things you can see right now. Write the noun, too.

Your turn to write

Draw something you really like. Write a sentence underneath.
Circle the nouns.

Capital letters and full stops

A sentence starts with a **capital letter**. It ends with a **full stop**.

The festival

Last weekend, I went to a festival for the very first time.

There were lots of people.

I went with Mum and Liam.

We had Turkish food. It was fun.

by Cameron

Beginning Who? When? Where?

Sequence of events things that happened in order

Ending how the writer feels

1 Finish these sentences and add the full stop.

a I am a ______________ (girl, boy)

b I like ______________ (birds, cats)

c I can ______________ (dance, run)

2 Choose a word from the box to start these sentences. Circle the capital letter in the word.

a ___ ___ ___ ___ are very little.

b ___ ___ ___ ___ go very fast.

Cars Apples Ants

c ___ ___ ___ ___ ___ ___ are very yummy.

To the teacher

Write a series of simple sentences without using capital letters and full stops. Ask the children if they notice anything wrong with them. Once they know what's missing, let them be the teacher and correct the sentences, using a different colour. This is an enjoyable way to reinforce this basic concept.

Recounts relate chronologically a series of past events in order to inform the reader.

Sentences

A **sentence** is one idea. This is a sentence.

Capital letter → **That is a big dog.** ← *Full stop*

3 You be the teacher! Use a red pencil. Tick the correct sentences. Fix the wrong ones.

a I am six

b the cat is fat.

c Look at the bug.

d Here is a big hat

e a fish swims in the sea

f He has red socks.

g she has a teddy.

h It is a soft koala

4 Write a sentence for each picture.

____

____

____

____

____

____

Your turn to write

Draw a picture of an interesting place you've been with your family. Write a sentence about it. Remember the capital letter and full stop.

Grammar focus

Proper nouns – people and places

Literary recount

Proper nouns are special nouns with capital letters.

Grandma Poss

Melbourne

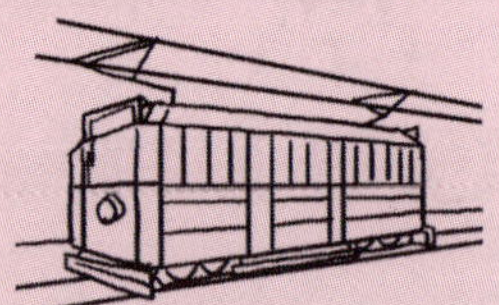

Possum Magic

← Title

Grandma Poss and Hush went all around Australia. ← **Beginning** Who? Where?

They got salad in Sydney. They got minties in Melbourne. And they got pavlova in Perth. ← **Sequence of events** Some main ideas

1 Write the names of the two main characters in the book.

a ____ u s h

b ____ r a n d m a ____ o s s

Write the name of the country they were in.

c  A ____ ____ t ____ ____ l i a

Write the names of two cities they went to.

d M ____ l ____ ____ ____ ____ n e

e S ____ d ____ ____ y

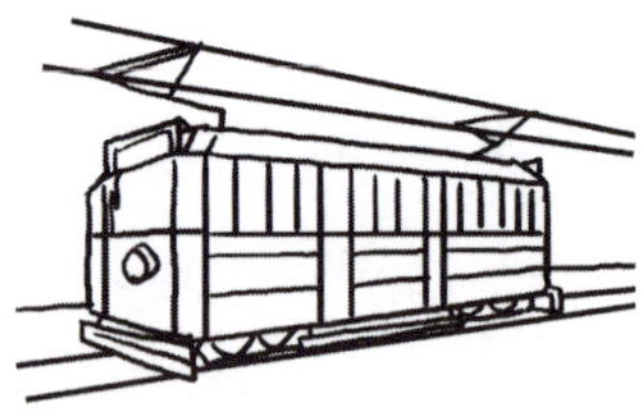

2 Write your name and where you live. Don't forget the capital letters.

Name ______________________________

I live in ______________________________

To the teacher

Get the children to write their own names. Point out that everyone's name is special so they all have capital letters. They can swap names and practise using capital letters by writing others' names. Help the children write their town or suburb. Brainstorm other places they know, listing them on the board and showing the use of capital letters (see next page). Make sentences – for example, Jacob lives in Darwin.

This literary recount takes the form of a retelling of a well-known children's story.

Unit 4

These are proper nouns: Australia  Sydney  Melbourne 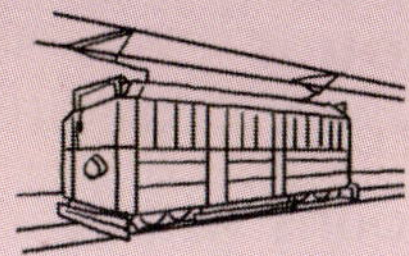

3 Draw three people you know. Write their names.

4 Draw three places you know. Write their names.

5 Now make some sentences using names of people and places.
For example, *Angus lives in Boronia*.

Your turn to write

Draw your family. Write each person's name under their pictures.
Now write where you live.

Proper nouns – days and months

Proper nouns are special nouns with capital letters.

Wednesday

April

An invitation

Title

Dear Grandpa,

Introduction

Please come to our special Grandparent's Day at school on Wednesday the 10th of April.

What is happening and why

We want to hear your stories about school.
We will have games and yummy food.

I hope you can come!

End statement

Love Daniel. xx

1 Write the days of the week. Every one starts with a capital letter. Use the Word bank to help you.

Sunday

M ____________________

____

Wednesday

____

____

____

Word bank

Friday
Tuesday
Saturday
Monday
Thursday

2 When do these events happen? Draw a line to the correct month.

Christmas	January
Grandparent's Day	April
The first month of the year is	December

To the teacher

Write the days of the week on cards and give one card each to seven children. Get the children to line up in the correct order of the days of the week. Invite discussion about what they do on different days of the week. Then use a birthday chart to discover when the children have birthdays. Write the months on the board with the names beside them. Point out the capital letters for days, months and people's names.

A transaction is to negotiate an agreement with someone else.

These are proper nouns: **S**unday 

Monday 

Friday 

3 Finish these sentences with proper nouns.

a Today is ________________________.

b Tomorrow will be ________________________.

c It is the month of ________________________.

d Next month will be ________________________.

4 What do you think? Finish these sentences.

a The best day of the week is ________________________.

I like it because ____

b The best month of the year is ________________________.

I like it because ____

5 Find some days and months in this Wordsearch.

Word list

Months
April
March
May
June
July
October

Days
Sunday
Tuesday
Friday

S	M	A	R	C	H	X
U	X	P	J	U	N	E
N	F	R	I	D	A	Y
D	X	I	X	M	A	Y
A	Y	L	J	U	L	Y
Y	A	D	S	E	U	T
O	C	T	O	B	E	R

Your turn to write

Draw some party pictures on some coloured paper. Then write an invitation to your birthday. Remember to put the day and the month of your party.

Plural nouns
Plural means more than one

cars 

trains 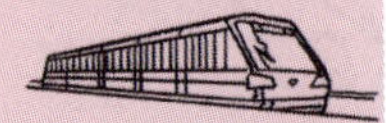

planes 

Transport

What is to be explained →
How do people travel?

Explanation of how →
Some people walk.
Some people ride bikes.
Some people drive cars to work.
Some people go to work in trains and buses.
Some people travel a long way on ships and planes.

1 Draw a circle around all of the plural nouns in the text. Now, copy each word and add s to make the noun plural.

tram		trams	
bike		b	
taxi		t	
ship			
truck			
hot-air balloon		hot-air	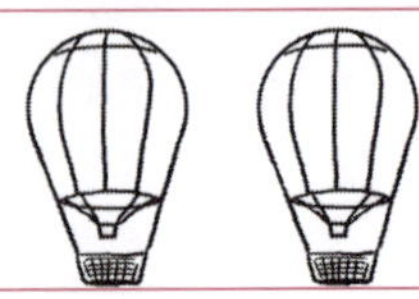
plane			

To the teacher

Before you complete this page, brainstorm types of transport. Ask the children to select one mode of transport and explain why they would choose to travel that way. Begin the sentence with the form of transport. For example, 'Trucks are good for taking petrol to the petrol station,' thereby using the plural noun.

An explanation clarifies how or why things happen, or how something works or has formed.

These are plural nouns: cars  helicopters 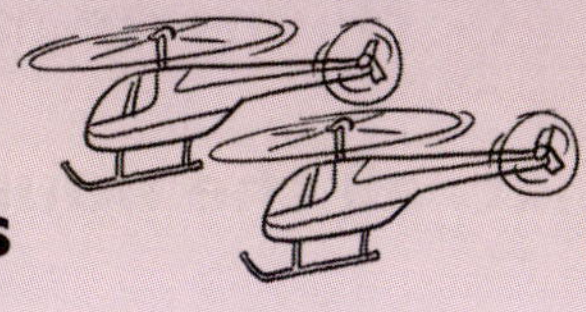 boats 

2 Choose a plural noun from the Word bank to finish these sentences.

a Look at those  ______________________!

b There are lots of  ______________________ on the tree.

c Jo has a tub of 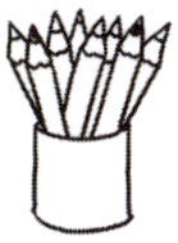 ______________________.

d Here is a bunch of  ______________________.

e The  ______________________ are for sale.

f Adam's  ______________________ are very loud!

Word bank

grapes
pencils
cats
drums
bugs
hats

3 Fill in the labels correctly. Add s to each word to make plural nouns.

Your turn to write

How do you choose your clothes? Draw your favourite clothes and write an explanation for when you would wear them.

Review

Nouns

Nouns are naming words

1 Write, in the hat, all the nouns we wear. Use the Word bank.

Word bank

 run

 shoes

 hat

 eyes

 jumper

 scarf

 teddy

 socks

 sit

Sentences

Sentences start with a capital letter and end with a full stop.

2 Write these sentences again. Put in the capital letters and full stops.

a the sun is very hot

____

b we played at the park

____

c look at that red car

____

Proper nouns

Proper nouns always have a capital letter.

3 Write some proper nouns you know.

a Two **people** you know ______________ ______________

b Two **places** you know ______________ ______________

c Two **days** you know ______________ ______________

d Two **months** you know ______________ ______________

(Do they all start with a capital letter?)

4 Write:

The name of your school ______________________________

Your auntie's name ______________________________

Plural nouns

Plural means more than one.

5 Write the plural of these words.

one rabbit

five rabbits

one car

three ______________

one dog

lots of ______________

one pen
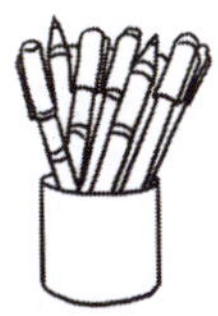
a tub of ______________

one duck

a family of ______________

one star

a million ______________

Adjectives

Adjectives are describing words.

little rectangle

black arrow

What am I?

I am a road sign.
I have two words.
I am a little rectangle.
I am black and white.
I have a black arrow.

by Katie

Title

What is being described

Describing features

1 Read the clues again and answer these questions.

a How many words are on the sign? ______________________

b What colour is the arrow? ______________________

c Where would you see the sign? ______________________

2 Look at this road sign. Draw a circle around the adjectives that you could use to describe it.

two numbers red small

circle

black round

square blue

To the teacher

Take the children out to a road near the school to look at the road signs. Ask them to choose a road sign to draw and then write three or four clues about it, using words to describe its colour, shape, size and purpose. They can then read their description of a sign to the grade for the others to guess the sign while still sitting in sight of it.

A description provides characteristic features of the subject.

These are adjectives.

old man  tall man  hot drink 

3 Write two adjectives to describe each thing.

____
____

____
____

____
____

____
____

4 Write an adjective from the picture before each noun.

a The clown has a __ __ __ __ __ __ hat.

b He has a __ __ __ __ neck.

c He has a __ __ __ __ nose.

d He has __ __ __ __ arms.

e He has a __ __ __ __ __ __ top.

f He has __ __ __ __ __ trousers

g He has very __ __ __ feet.

Your turn to write

Draw your favourite food – think about what it looks like and tastes like. Is it hot or cold, crunchy or soft? Write a sentence to describe it.

Adjectives

An **adjective** is a describing word.

huge

little

black

fat

The Giant

Jack was hiding. He saw the giant.

The giant was huge!
He had little, black eyes and a fat belly. He had big feet and sharp, yellow teeth.

The giant didn't see Jack.

Who is being described

Describing features

1 Write the adjectives from the text that describe these things:

a b __ __ feet 

b l __ __ __ __ __, b __ __ __ __ eyes 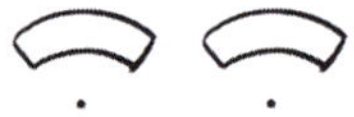

c f __ __ belly 

d s __ __ __ __, y __ __ __ __ __ teeth 

2 What do you think Jack looked like? Write two sentences to describe Jack.

____

____

____

____

Now draw the giant to match the description!

To the teacher

In pairs, ask the children to look carefully at a partner – their hair, eyes, teeth, skin, height, clothing and special features such as moles, birthmarks, earrings, glasses. Ask them to draw their partner and write a simple description underneath. They could also describe YOU!

A description includes some of the features of particular people, places or things.

These are adjectives: black  fat  little 

3 Circle the words that describe something in this picture. Cross out the ones that don't.

long spotty new metal bare dead big wooden tall

wet grey short happy little thin dark dirty

4 Fill the gaps. Use the adjectives in the picture to help.

a Jane is a _ _ _ _ _ girl.

b It is a _ _ _ _ _ day.

c She has a _ _ _ , _ _ _ _ _ umbrella.

d She has a _ _ _ _ raincoat.

e There are some _ _ _ _ _ puddles.

f Jane splashes through the puddles in her _ _ _ _ _ gumboots.

Your turn to write

What is your favourite thing to play with, play in or play on? It might be a toy, a bike, a trampoline, a cubby or a sandpit. Write a description of it and draw a picture of it on the back. See if a friend can guess what it is.

Pronouns are used to replace a noun.

I
her
she
me

The tooth fairy

I saw my tooth fairy.
I like her and she likes me.
I made a fairy garden.
My sister helped me.
I love it.

by Taiya

← **Beginning** Who? What?
← **Sequence of events** things that happened in order
← **How the writer feels**

1 Use the Word bank. Fill the gaps with pronouns.

a ____ saw the tooth fairy.

b I like ____ ____ ____.

c ____ ____ ____ likes me.

d My sister helped ____ ____.

Word bank

she her I me

2 Circle the pronouns in these sentences.

a She has new shoes.

b I can see the hungry lion.

c Mum took me to the shops.

3 Now use these words to write your own sentences.

She ____________________

I ____________________

To the teacher

The use of pronouns is a difficult concept for young children to grasp, even though they use them in their speech frequently. Ask them to think of an interesting person (famous or personal) and explain their reasons for their interest. Identify the pronouns they use and make a list of these pronouns and the words they replace.

Recounts relate chronologically a series of past events in order to inform the reader.

These are pronouns: he  she  it 

4 Choose the correct pronoun to complete these sentences. For example:

<u>He</u> will play with me at lunchtime.
(He, It)

a ______________ are going to play after school.
(We, It)

b During the storm ______________ blew off.
(it, she)

c ______________ is a great reader!
(He, They)

d What did you say to ______________?
(them, he)

e ______________ are making a lot of noise!
(They, Her)

5 Match the pronoun with these pictures. Draw a line to join the words.

she he they it

Your turn to write

Have you lost a tooth? Write about your tooth fairy experience. Use your imagination if you haven't lost one yet!

Verbs are doing words.

eat is a doing word

wag is a doing word

brush is a doing word

Chocolate the calf

← Title

Calves eat grass and wag their tails to brush the flies away.

← Describing features

1 What else can cows **do**? Draw a picture to go with the first **verb**, and then think of two more things a cow can do.

sleep

2 What are three things **YOU** can do? Write and draw them here.

smile

To the teacher

Children love to play *Simon says*. Play the game outside. Tell the children to remember what they do during the game. You could include some miming. For example, Simon says, "Follow the emu tracks", "Climb the tree", "Sit next to the river". At the end of the game, brainstorm the actions and get the children to identify the verbs. **Note:** Use the illustrations to revise nouns.

A description is a series of facts about the topic.

These are verbs:

walk  eat  wag 

3 Find a word in the Word bank below to finish these sentences. They are all verbs.

a First I ____ ____ ____ out of bed.

b Next I ____ ____ ____ on my clothes.

c I know how to ____ ____ ____ my shoelaces.

d Mum always tells me to ____ ____ ____ ____ ____ my hair.

e I ____ ____ ____ a big bowl of porridge.

f I ____ ____ ____ ____ Mum a big kiss and say, "Goodbye!"

Word bank

eat put give get brush tie

4 Use these verbs in a sentence:

play ____

____

eat ____

____

Your turn to write

Draw your own pet OR a pet you would like to have. Write a description of what it eats, where it sleeps and what it **does**. For example, you could describe the games it plays, the noises it makes and how it moves. Then underline the words that describe what it does. These words are verbs.

Present tense verbs are doing words that tell what is happening now.

sits
eating
comes
say

Little Miss Muffet

Little Miss Muffet,
Sits on her tuffet
Eating her curds and whey.
Along comes a spider
And sits down beside her
What does Miss Muffet say?

← **Title**

← **Rhyming words**
muffet
tuffet
whey
say
spider
her

1 Draw Miss Muffet sitting and the spider coming down beside her. Write what Miss Muffet says in the speech bubble.

2 Draw pictures to show what is happening now.

I **play** with my friends.	Dogs **run** fast.

To the teacher

Play *What are you doing?* Children stand in a circle. One child might pretend to tie her shoelaces, for example. The next child asks, "What are you doing?" The first child answers, "Tying my shoelaces." The next child does something different – for example, pretends to make a cake. The next child in the circle asks what the next person is doing. This continues around the circle. At the end, brainstorm the present tense verbs that were used.

These are present tense verbs:

sits  eating  saying 

3 Many present tense verbs have ing on the end.
Write the correct verb from the Word bank to fill the gap.

a Amy is ___ ___ ___ ___ ___ ___ ___ bubbles. 

b Callum is ___ ___ ___ ___ ___ ___ ___ the drum. 

c Tan is ___ ___ ___ ___ ___ ___ ___ a ball. 

d Maria is ___ ___ ___ ___ ___ ___ ___ the dog. 

e Nathan is ___ ___ ___ ___ ___ ___ loudly. 

Word bank

patting
blowing
crying
kicking
beating

4 Look around your classroom.
Write what some people are doing right now.

a I am ______________________________________ .

b My teacher is ______________________________________ .

c ______________________________________ .

d ______________________________________ .

5 Think of two things you wish you were doing right now.
Draw a picture of them.

Your turn to write

Imagine you are at the shops. Draw a picture to show what is happening and write a sentence or two about it. Use **ing** verbs. For example: The lady is **looking** in the window.

Past tense verbs are doing words that have already happened.

lost

shouted

stayed

Lost in the big shops

I was lost at the shops. I could not find Mum.

"Mum! Mum!" I shouted.

She didn't answer.

"Mum!" I was scared.

I found her. She was in the clothes section again!

Then I stayed with her the whole time.

Beginning Who? Where?

Sequence of events things that happened

Ending

1 Look at the recount again to help you to finish these sentences. Write the correct words in a sentence.

I was ____ ____ ____ ____ at the shops.

"Mum! Mum!" I ____ ____ ____ ____ ____ ____ ____.

2 Write these words in one sentence: was happy

____

3 Add ed to these words.

"Dad! Dad!" I yell____ ____.

I stay____ ____ with Mum.

The big dog bark____ ____.

4 Write ed words to match the pictures.

jump____ ____

sail ____ ____

cook____ ____

To the teacher

Talk about weekend or holiday activities. List the past tense verbs the children use. Draw attention to the times they used 'was' and words they used which end in 'ed'. Emphasise that they used the verbs this way because they are **past tense – they've already happened.**

Recounts relate chronologically a series of past events in order to inform the reader.

These are past tense verbs:

shouted  found  stayed 

5 Change the word is to was in the sentences below.
For example:

Mia is asleep. — **Mia was asleep.**

a Tom is lost. — Tom ____ ____ ____ lost.

b Olivia is sick. — Olivia ____ ____ ____ sick.

c The dog is noisy. — The dog ____ ____ ____ noisy.

d The train is fast. — The train ____ ____ ____ fast.

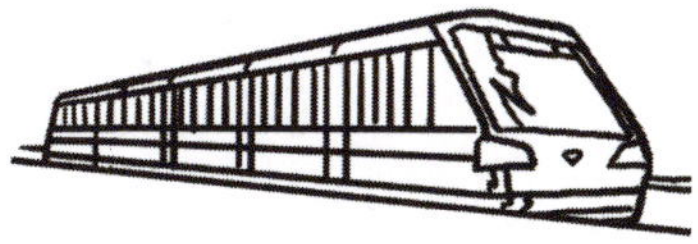

6 Finish these sentences by adding ed to the end of the verbs.

 lick	He **licked** the chocolate ice-cream.
 wash	Mum ____ ____ ____ ____ ____ ____ the muddy car.
 play	After school Emily ____ ____ ____ ____ ____ ____ at my house.
 look	Sam ____ ____ ____ ____ ____ ____ for his lost ball.
 walk	The old cat ____ ____ ____ ____ ____ ____ with a limp.

7 Write about something you did last week. Circle the verb.

Last week I ______________________________

Your turn to write

Write about a time when you were lost. Or you can make up a story about someone who got lost at the zoo. Draw a picture to show where you (or the character in your story) were found.

Adjectives

Adjectives tell us more about nouns.
For example: I am a little, furry, grey mouse with big, round ears.

1 Circle the adjectives. There are two in each sentence.

a  This is a big, yummy Easter egg.

b  Tom ate the cold vanilla ice-cream.

c  He climbed up the steep, rocky mountain.

d  The huge, white bird flew across the sky.

e  Con saw a new, speedy car.

Pronouns

Pronouns take the place of nouns.
Some pronouns are: he she me I it

2 Choose a pronoun to write in the space.

a When Jordan patted the cat __________ purred.
(us, it, we)

b Mum gave __________ a salad roll for my lunch.
(me, they, you)

c __________ played basketball after school.
(us, them, I)

d After __________ got home, Sally had a bath.
(he, she, it)

e Sam said __________ would ride his bike to school.
(it, us, he)

Unit 14

Verbs

Verbs are doing words. I'm jumping!

3 Circle the verbs below to show what ducks do.

swim   quack
eat
feathers   waddle   him
eggs   peck
water   dive   farm
fly
sleep   hide   scratch

There are 10 verbs. Did you get them all?

4 Write a verb to show what these animals can do.

a  A snake can ____________________.

b  A kangaroo can ____________________.

c  A koala can ____________________.

d  A kookaburra can ____________________.

e  A shark can ____________________.

Word bank

laugh
jump
swim
hiss
climb

5 Write some sentences to show what you can do.

a At home I can ____.

b At school I can ____.

c On the holidays I can ____________________________________.

Now circle the verbs you used.

Adverbs

Adverbs add meaning to verbs.

Verb	Adverb
fly	swiftly
climb	quickly

How animals move

Animals move in different ways.
Kangaroos bound easily.
Platypus swim smoothly.
Hawks fly swiftly.
Wombats waddle heavily.
Koalas climb quickly.
Animals move the best way they can!

← Title
← Introduces the topic
← Series of facts
← Ending

1 Look at the information report.
Add the adverbs to show how the animals move.

a Wombats waddle ____________________.

b Platypus swim ____________________.

c Kangaroos bound ____________________.

d Koalas climb ____________________.

e Hawks fly ____________________.

2 Use an adverb from the Word bank to finish these sentences.

a  Tricia cried ____________________.

b  Sam rode his skateboard ____________________.

c  Harry read his book ____________________.

Word bank
quietly
loudly
carefully

To the teacher

Play *Simon says* using adverbs. For example: walk silently, bob up and down quickly, turn slowly, wave happily, nod excitedly, clap loudly, tip-toe softly.
Ask how a baby eats, walks, sleeps, laughs, cries, claps. Make comparisons with how the children in your class do these things using adverbs. Then compare with adults – for example, who sleep noisily (snore loudly!).

Answer pages

Unit 1

1 a picnic **b** friends **c** branch **d** chin
2 Teacher **3** hat, apple, egg, carl, socks, pig
4 bike, hat, Teacher to correct 'I am a pet.'

Unit 2

1 a cheese **b** meat **c** pizza **d** pineapple
2 Teacher **3** Teacher **4** Teacher

Unit 3

1 Teacher **2 a** Ants **b** Cars **c** Apples
3 Teacher **4** Teacher **5** Teacher

Unit 4

1 a Hush **b G**randma **P**oss **c** Australia
d Melbourne **e** Sydney **2** Teacher
3 Teacher **4** Teacher

Unit 5

1 Sunday, **M**onday, **T**uesday, Wednesday, **T**hursday, **F**riday, **S**aturday **2** Christmas – **December** Grandparent's Day – **April**
The first month of the year is **January**
3 Teacher **4** Teacher **5** Teacher

Unit 6

1 trams, bikes, taxis, ships, trucks, hot-air balloons, planes **2 a** cats **b** bugs **c** pencils **d** grapes **e** hats **f** drums **3** legs, hands, eyes, noses, arms, friends, shoes

Unit 7

1 shoes, hat, jumper, scarf, socks
2 a The sun is very hot. **b** We played at the park. **c** Look at that red car.
3 Teacher **4** Teacher **5** three cars, lots of dogs, a tub of pens, a family of ducks, a million stars

Unit 8

1 a two **b** black **c** on the road **2** two, red, small, black, round **3** Teacher
4 a The clown has a **pointy** hat. **b** He has a **thin** neck. **c** He has a **pink** nose. **d** He has **long** arms. **e** He has a **spotty** top. **f** He has **baggy** trousers. **g** He has very **big** feet.

Unit 9

1 a big feet **b** little, black eyes **c** fat belly **d** sharp, yellow teeth **2** Teacher **3** Circled words – long, spotty, metal, bare, dead, big, wooden, wet, grey, happy, little, thin, dirty **4 a** happy **b** rainy **c** big, black **d** warm **e** muddy **f** shiny

Unit 10

1 a I **b** her **c** She **d** me **2** Circle – she, I, me. **3** Teacher **4 a** We **b** it **c** He **d** them **e** They **5** Teacher

Unit 11

1 Teacher **2** Teacher **3** got, put, tie, brush, eat, give **4** Teacher

Unit 12

1 Teacher **2** Teacher **3 a** blowing **b** beating **c** kicking **d** patting **e** crying
4 Teacher **5** Teacher

Unit 13

1 lost, shouted **2** Teacher **3** yelled, stayed, barked **4** jumped, sailed, cooked **5 a** was **b** was **c** was **d** was **6** licked, washed, played, looked, walked **7** Teacher

Unit 14

1 big, yummy; cold, vanilla; steep, rocky; huge, white new, speedy **2 a** it **b** me **c** I **d** she **e** he **3** swim, quack, eat, waddle, sleep, fly, hide, scratch, dive, peck **4** hiss, jump, climb, laugh, swim **5** Teacher

Unit 15

1 a heavily **b** smoothly **c** easily **d** quickly **e** swiftly **2 a** loudly **b** carefully **c** quietly **3 a** loudly **b** brightly **c** suddenly **d** badly **e** dangerously **f** bravely **4** listen carefully, eat greedily, sleep deeply, swim strongly, write neatly, talk loudly **5** Teacher

Unit 16

1 Teacher **2 a** along **b** through **c** beside **d** in **e** over **f** down **3** Teacher

Unit 17

1 Circle **a** H, **b** T **c** T **d** S **2** Teacher **3 a** saw **b** chased **c** ran **4 a** jumped **b** mooed **c** growled **d** climbed **e** purred **f** galloped **5** Teacher **6** Teacher

Unit 18

1 Teacher **2** Teacher **3** Teacher **4** Teacher **5 6 a** What games will we play? **b** Is that the doorbell? **c** What am I going to wear? **d** When will they be here? **7** Teacher

Unit 19

1 Teacher **2** Teacher **3** Teacher **4** Teacher

Unit 20

1 a can't **b** It's **c** She's **d** Don't **e** We're **f** Let's **g** I'm **h** He's **2** do not – don't, let us – let's, he is – he's, can not – can't, she is – she's, It is – It's, we are – we're, I am – I'm **3 a** I'm **b** isn't **c** we're **d** didn't **e** let's **4** Teacher

Unit 21

1 The boy is hiding **in** the box. Harry slept **under** the blankets. The sandwich is **between** the banana and the milk. The trailier is **behind** the tractor. **2** Teacher **3** Teacher **4** Teacher **5 a** Let's **b** doesn't **c** isn't **d** can't **e** We're

Unit 22

1 Teacher **2 a** and **b** because **c** because **d** and **3** Teacher **4 a** so **b** and **c** but **d** because **e** so **f** but **5** He felt happy **so** he sang a song. The dog scratched Toby **but** it didn't hurt. Pop's car was shiny **because** it had just been washed. We had a picnic in the park **and** went for a walk, too. Scott burnt his mouth **because** the soup was hot! It was time to go **so** I said, "Goodbye!" **6** Teacher

Unit 23

1 a Place **b** Push **c** Put **d** Spray **e** Stand **f** see **2** good – excellent, great; small – little tiny; bad – rotten, naughty; yelled – shouted, screamed **3** thin/skinny, run/jog, mug/cup, sea/ocean, cry/sob, cool/cold **4 a** road **b** Throw **c** dish **d** pretty **e** students **f** present (Other suggestions may be acceptable) **5** Teacher

Unit 24

1 up/down, hot/cold, new/old, tall/short, boy/girl, yes/no **2** A kettle is hot but a fridge is cold. **3** Teacher **4** Teacher

Unit 25

1 First an egg is laid on a leaf. **Then** a caterpillar hatches out. **Next** the caterpillar spins a cocoon. **Finally** a butterfly is born. **2** Teacher **3** Teacher **4** Jon, Emu, Duck

Unit 26

1 sunshine, backbone **2 a** bedroom **b** weekend **c** football **d** outside **e** armchair **f** blackberry **3** and **4** ladybird, bathroom, teaspoon, raincoat, handbag, everyone, cannot, grandmother **5 a** butterfly **b** bathroom **c** raincoat **6** Teacher

Unit 27

1 a The dog said, "Woof!" **b** The cow said, "Moo!" **c** The sheep said, "Baa!" **d** The dove said, "Coo!" **2 a** My teacher said, "Do you need help?" **b** Corey said, "It's lunchtime soon." **c** "Hurry up!" Mum said **d** Curtis said, "I'm going to ride my bike." **e** "Look at that big lizard!" said Sophie. **f** Little piggy-wig said, "I'm running back to my sty!" **3 a** The horse said, "Neigh!" **b** The farmer said, "It's a lovely day!" **c** The sheep said, "Baa!" **d** The rooster said, "Cock-a-doodle-doo!" **e** The lady said, "Good horse!" **f** The cow said, "Moo!" **g** The boy said, "Look at me!" **4** Teacher

Unit 28

1 a because **b** but **c** and **d** so **2 a** small **b** cold **c** scared **d** jog **e** look **f** crash **g** glad **h** fib **3 a** girl **b** slowly **c** yes **d** dirty **e** day **f** happy **4** First, Next, Then, Finally **5 a** basketball **b** toothbrush **c** eyelash **d** inside **e** watermelon **f** forever **6** "Oh dear," said Mother Bear. "Someone has been in our house," said Father Bear. "Look at the table!" said Baby Bear. "Someone's been eating my porridge," said Father Bear. "Someone's been eating my porridge," said Mother Bear. "Someone's been eating my porridge," said Baby Bear. "And they've eaten it all up!"

Unit 29

1 white, When, wind, walk, White, Where **2** washing, went, wing, window, with **3** and **4** Funny Fred fries footy franks on Fridays. Can the crazy cockatoo catch the clever caterpillar? "Mmm," mumbled Monty Mouse. "My Mum makes yummy mushies!" **5** Teacher

Unit 30

1 Teacher **2** rain – tinkles, sprinkles, splishes, splashes wind – bustles, rustles, hums, strums hail – bangs, twangs, clatters, patters thunder – rumbles, grumbles, bashes, crashes RUSTLE, rustle, rustle, SWISH, swish, swishshshshshsh …
3 Teacher

Unit 15

These are adverbs: fly swift**ly**  climb quick**ly** 

3 Draw a circle around the ly adverbs in these sentences.

a Mum cheered loudly during the race. 

b The sun shone brightly. 

c Kristy stopped suddenly when she saw the fast car. 

d The work was done badly. 1 + 3 = 5 ✗; 9 − 7 = 3 ✗; 8 + 4 = 11 ✗

e The snake hissed dangerously. 

f Ryan watched bravely as the doctor put plaster on his broken leg. 

**4 Think of a way you can do these things.
Write a suitable adverb after the verb.**

 listen ____________________  eat ____________________

 sleep ____________________  swim ____________________

 write ____________________  talk ____________________

Word bank

greedily
carefully
loudly
neatly
deeply
strongly

**5 Write a sentence about something you like to do.
Use an adverb to show <u>how</u> you do it.**

____

____

Your turn to write

Think of the way another animal moves. Draw a picture of it and write a sentence about how it moves.

Prepositions tell us where something is.

Pancake recipe

Heading

You will need:

What you need – list of ingredients

1 cup flour 1½ cups milk
2 eggs butter for frying

You will need to ask an adult to help with steps 4, 5 and 6.

What to do:

Steps – instructions in numbered steps

1 Put flour into a bowl. (*into a bowl*)
2 Add the eggs with some of the milk and stir it through.
3 Add the rest of the milk to the mixture and stir. (*to the mixture*)
4 Heat butter in the frying pan. (*in the frying pan*)
5 Drop batter in large spoonfuls into the pan.
6 When the top bubbles put egg lifter under the pancake and flip it over. (*under the pancake*)
7 When both sides are golden, add your favourite topping and eat!

The words *into*, *in*, *under* are prepositions.

1 Try this word puzzle. The words are prepositions from the recipe.

Across

2 Heat butter **i**_____ the pan.
3 Stir the milk and eggs **t**_______________.
5 Put the egg lifter **u**__________ the pancake.

Down

1 Add the eggs **w**__________ some of the milk.
2 Put the flour **i**________ the bowl.
4 Flip the pancake **o**__________.

							1 w
	2 i	n					i
	n						t
	3 t	h	r	4 o	u	g	h
	o			v			
				e			
5 u	n	d	e	r			

To the teacher

Play *Where are we?* For example, you say, "Beside!" The children place themselves 'beside' another person or thing. Ask them to say where they are in a sentence. Continue with other prepositions, such as under, between, against, inside. Identify these words as prepositions.

Unit 16

These are prepositions:

Put the milk **into** the bowl.

Toss the pancake **over**.

2 Choose a preposition from the Word bank to fill the gaps.

a  The car went ____________ the road.

b  The plane flew ____________ the air.

c  The lamp sat ____________ the clock.

d  The children were sitting ________ the bus.

e  He carried the boat ____________ his head.

f  Marc got ____________ his knees.

Word bank

over
through
in
beside
along
on

3 Draw this picture. Follow the instructions carefully. The bold words are prepositions.

- Draw a shark **in** the middle of the space.

- Add a big rock and some seaweed **under** him.
- Add water all **around** him.
- Draw a big octopus **beside** him.
- Draw three fish **near** his mouth.

Your turn to write

Write some instructions to a friend asking them to draw a picture. Tell your friend what is in the picture and where the characters are. For example on a farm, at a circus, at school, at home . . .

Sentences always make sense.

The lion and the mouse

Title

Beginning
Who? What?

One day, the king of the lions was asleep in his den.

Middle
What happened next?

Sentences always start with a capital letter.

The mouse saw the lion. She skittered up to it. She hit the lion on the head with a rolling pin.

Ending

The lion chased the mouse. The mouse ran away.

by Taiya

Author

1 Sentences <u>always</u> start with a capital letter. Circle the capital letters in these sentences.

a He was asleep.

b The lion is the king.

c The mouse is tiny.

d She saw the lion.

2 In this passage, the sentences always have a full stop. Circle the <u>full stops</u> in the sentences above.

3 Sentences always have <u>a verb</u> (an action or doing word). Write in the action words:

a The mouse s ____ ____ the lion.

b The lion c ____ ____ ____ ____ ____ the mouse.

c The mouse r ____ ____ away.

To the teacher

Refer back to Unit 3 when full stops and capital letters were introduced. Emphasise that a sentence must always make sense and must always have a verb.

A narrative is an entertaining story that has a beginning (Who? What?), relates a series of events, has a middle and ends with a concluding sentence.

Is this a sentence?

Leo the lion	No, it does not have a verb.
Leo the lion roared.	Yes, it has a verb. Write the verb. **r** ___ ___ ___ ___ ___

4 Finish off the sentences below. Use the verbs from the Verb box.

a  Freddie the frog j________________.

b  Daisy the cow m________________.

c  Fido the dog g________________.

d  Poss the koala c________________.

e  Lily the cat p________________.

f  Billy the horse g________________.

Verb box

mooed
growled
climbed
purred
jumped
galloped

5 Write a sentence of your own. Choose a verb from the Verb box.

____

6 Draw a picture of the lion and the mouse.
Write a verb to tell what the lion did.

____

Your turn to write

Write your own story about your favourite animal. Make sure it has a beginning, a middle and an ending.

Questions

A question asks something.

How does a car work?

How does a car work?

These are the parts to help a car move.

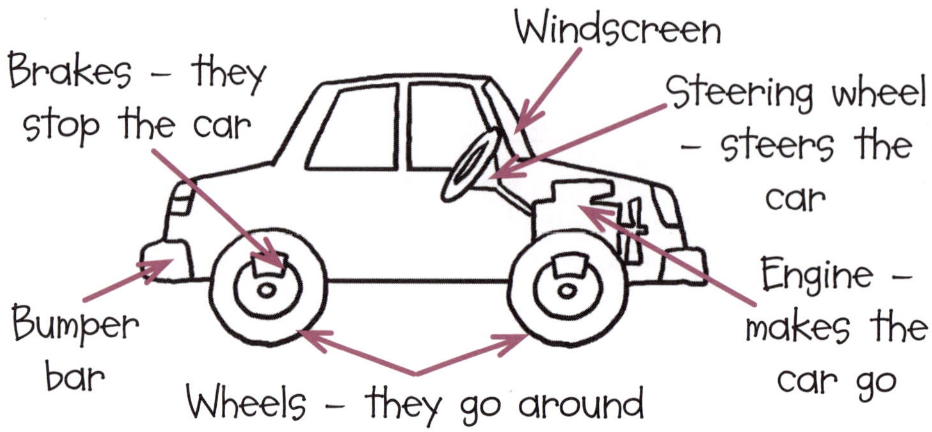

If the engine stops, the car can't go.

Title

What is to be explained

Explanation telling how

Ending

1 Look at the explanation again. Match the answers to the questions.

What does the engine do?
What do the brakes do?
What do the wheels do?
What does the steering wheel do?

They stop the car.
It makes the car go.
It steers the car.
They go around.

2 A question always has a question mark. ?
Write in the missing question marks. Then answer the questions.

a What is your name? ____________________

b How old are you ____________________

c Are you a boy or a girl? ____________________

d What colour are your eyes ____________________

e Do you have a pet ____________________

To the teacher

Have a Question box in your classroom to encourage children to express their natural curiosity as they learn. Select one question each day to discuss, research or to be shared at home and re-visited the next day at school.

These are questions: How does a car work? What is that?

This is a question mark.

3 Read this story with a friend.

It was Andy's 7th birthday. He was so excited because he was having a party. All his friends were coming.
"What will we have to eat, Mum?" asked Andy.
"What games will we play, Dad?" he asked.
Andy asked, "What am I going to wear?"
"When will they be here?" he asked.
"What time is it?" Andy asked.
"Is that the doorbell?" Andy yelled.
"Yippee! It's time for my party to start!"

4 Circle all the question marks in this story.

5 How many questions does Andy ask? ________

6 Finish these questions from the story. Don't forget the question marks.

a What games ____________________

b Is that ____________________

c What am I ____________________

d When will ____________________

7 Write a question you would ask your mum and dad if you were having a party.

____

Your turn to write

Draw a picture of a bike. Label the parts of the bike and explain what they are used for. If you don't ride a bike, choose something else you know about to explain.

Exclamations are short comments or loud noises!

These are exclamation marks. !!!

The alien

← **Title**

One night when I was asleep a spaceship landed in my backyard. Whoosh!

← **Beginning** Who? When? Where?

An alien came out. It came into my house. It came into my room! It picked me up! It took me to the spaceship!

← **Middle** What happened?

And then it took me home again.

← **Ending**

by Jemma

These are exclamations:

Here is one exclamation from the story:

It took me to the spaceship!

1 Write the other three exclamations here. Use exclamation marks.

____

____

____

2 Draw yourself. Write what you would say if an alien landed in your yard. Use the speech bubble.

To the teacher

Discuss various scenarios with the children – if they fell into a river, saw a little child running onto the road, were hurt by someone, were lost at the shops … Ask the children to role play these situations and use appropriate expressions (exclamations). Make a list of what they say and use exclamation marks.

A narrative is an entertaining story that relates a series of events that pose a problem and a solution, played out by characters in a specific setting.

Exclamation marks

When you exclaim, you yell loudly and suddenly.
Exclamation marks show this in writing.

3 Here are some exclamations you might say. Put in the exclamation marks.

Look out for the snake

Wow

I'm so excited

I heard a strange noise

Let's go

You're mean

4 What are they saying? Write in these speech bubbles below. Don't forget the exclamation mark!

Your turn to write

Draw something scary. Now write a story about it.
Use exclamation marks if there are loud noises or shouting.

Contractions are when two words make one.

It's

I'm

he's

My puppy

It's funny
my puppy
knows just how I feel.

When I'm happy
he's yappy
and squirms like an eel.

When I'm grumpy
he's slumpy
and stays at my heel.

It's funny
my puppy
knows such a great deal.

by Aileen Fisher

← **Title**

← **Rhymes** *happy* *yappy*

← **Written in verses**

← **Poet**

These are contractions:

it + is = it's   I + am = I'm   he + is = he's
we + are = we're   do + not = don't

Where letters are left out, we use an apostrophe, which looks like this. ’

1 Circle the contractions in these sentences.

a Con can't run today.

b It's going to rain.

c She's a funny girl.

d Don't go home yet!

e We're finished.

f Let's have a drink.

g I'm hungry!

h He's all wet!

2 Draw a line between each contraction and the two words it means.

do not	let us	he is	can not	she is	It is	we are	I am
he's	don't	It's	let's	she's	we're	I'm	can't

To the teacher

Give the children the opportunity to look through some books they can read and identify some contractions. Ask them to copy the sentence and circle the contraction. See if they can write the two separate words underneath.

Poems vary in structure but are often written in verses and have rhyming words.

Contractions

Contractions are used when two words are shortened to make one word. For example: we are = we're

3 Do the word sum in the box. Drop the coloured letter and add an apostrophe ('). Then write it in the sentence. For example:

she + is = **she's**

She's using the computer.

I + am =

a ____________ having chicken for my dinner.

is + not =

b Dad says it ____________ going to rain today.

we + are =

c After school ____________ going to the park.

did + not =

d He ____________ catch a fish all day!

let + us =

e Ben said, "____________ go for a bike ride!"

4 Write your own sentences using these contractions.

can't ____

____

he's ____

____

don't ____

____

Your turn to write

Write a short poem about your own pet – or one that you would like to have. Use at least one contraction.

Prepositions

Prepositions tell us where things are.

1 Choose the correct preposition to finish each sentence.

 The boy is hiding	***between***	_____ the box.
 Harry slept	***in***	_______ the blankets.
 The sandwich is	***under***	_________ the banana and the drink.
 The trailer is	***behind***	_______ the tractor

2 Draw:

a a frog **in** the middle of the fishbowl

b water **around** the frog

c a water lily **under** the frog

d a fly **above** the frog

e tadpoles swimming **in** the water.

Questions

A **question** asks something.

3 Make up your own endings to these sentences. (Don't forget the question marks.)

a Do you want to ______________________________

b Will you please get me ______________________________

c When is the ______________________________

d How do you ______________________________

e What is ______________________________

Exclamation marks

An **exclamation** shows surprise, annoyance or pain. It can also mean a noise.

4 Write a comment from the Word bank to match the pictures. Use an exclamation mark.

Word bank

Splash! Bang! Bang! Look at me!
Pow! Wheeeeeee!

Contractions

Contractions are when two words are shortened make one word. For example: was not = wasn't

5 Replace the two bold words with one contraction from the Word bank. Use an apostrophe.

Word bank

can't
isn't
Let's
doesn't
We're

a **Let us** go to the city next weekend.

_____________ go to the city next weekend.

b Mitchell **does not** want to ride a horse.

Mitchell _____________ want to ride a horse.

c The dog **is not** going to bite you.

The dog _____________ going to bite you.

d I **can not** see any koalas in the tree.

I _____________ see any koalas in the tree.

e **We are** making some chocolate cakes.

_____________ making some chocolate cakes.

Conjunctions are joining words.

because

and

when

Things that make me happy ← Title

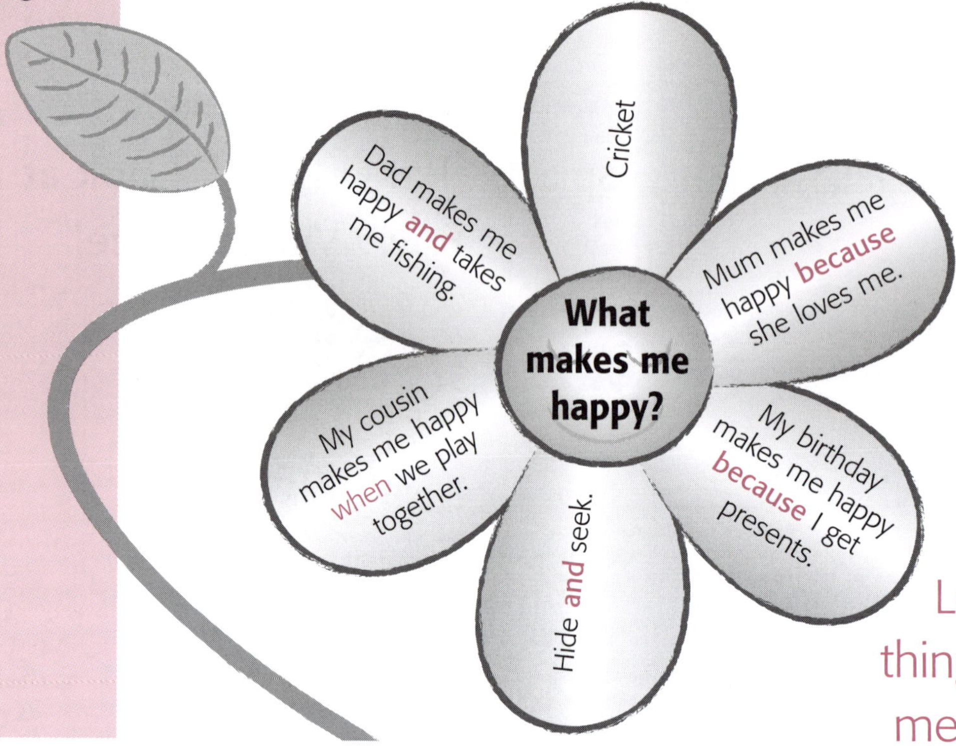

← What I think

Lots of things make me happy! ← Ending my opinion

1 Circle the words because, when and and in the petals of the flower.

2 Write because or and to finish these sentences.

a Dad makes me happy ____________ takes me fishing.

b My birthday makes me happy ____________ I get presents.

c Mum makes me happy ____________ she loves me.

d Nan makes me happy ____________ gives me hugs.

3 Now write about two things that make you happy and give a reason. Use because or and.

a ____

____

b ____

____

To the teacher

Conjunctions help children to extend their sentences orally and in writing. Instead of saying "It was fun", ask for a reason. They can then say "It was fun because . . ." and write it down. Conjunctions 'but', 'so' and 'and' can be used in the same way. For example, "We wanted to go to the park but it was too late."

These are conjunctions:

Dad makes me happy **and** takes me fishing.

My birthday makes me happy **because** I get presents.

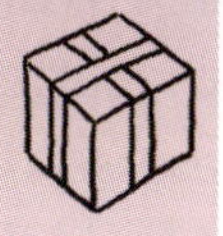

4 Circle and, so, but and because in these sentences.

- **a** It was cold so I put on my jacket.
- **b** Chelsea ate two big apples and three grapes.
- **c** We looked for ages but we couldn't find the ball.
- **d** Tate's pants were too short because he had grown.
- **e** The tyre was flat so I couldn't ride my bike.
- **f** Mum packed my bag but she forgot my teddy.

5 Draw a line to match the two parts of these sentences.

He felt happy	**because** it had just been washed.
The dog scratched Toby	**so** he sang a song.
Pop's car was shiny	**so** I said, "Goodbye!"
We had a picnic in the park	**but** it didn't hurt.
Scott burnt his mouth	**and** went for a walk, too.
It was time to go	**because** the soup was hot!

6 Write endings to these sentences.

I was tired so ______________________________

We didn't catch any fish but ______________________________

____

Your turn to write

Draw a picture of something you like to do. Write at least two sentences about why you think it's so much fun.
Give your reasons.

Synonyms

Synonyms are words that mean *the same or nearly the same.*

big – large

How to grow a seed

← **Heading**

You will need

← **What you need** list of materials

soil a pot

water seed – pumpkin or carrot

What to do

← **Steps** instructions in numbered steps

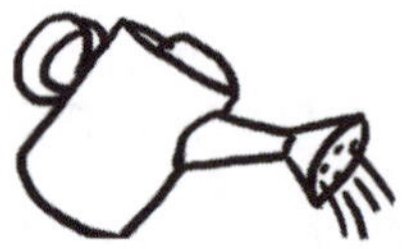

1 Put the soil into a pot.

2 Poke a hole in the soil with your fingers.

3 Drop the seed into the hole.

4 Sprinkle water over it.

5 Place it near a window so that it gets some sun.

6 Wait and watch it grow.

1 **Circle the synonym. One word in each step has been changed. Find it and circle it.**

a Place the soil into the pot.

b Push a hole into the soil with your finger.

c Put the seed into the hole.

d Spray water over it.

e Stand it near the window so that it gets the sun.

f Wait and see it grow.

2 **Circle two more words that mean the same.**

good	excellent	crayon	great	huge
small	table	little	tiny	clever
bad	rotten	car	excited	naughty
yelled	very	shouted	screamed	lovely

To the teacher

Give children the chance to think of synonyms that could be used to replace a particular word. For example, sprinkle, drizzle, water, shower could be used instead of spray.

Unit 23

These are synonyms: **big** = enormous, huge **clever** = smart, brainy **like** = love, enjoy **saw** = watched, looked at

3 Use the Word bank and write the words that mean the same next to the correct picture.

t______________

s______________

____

____

____

____

____

____

____

____

____

____

Word bank

cup	cool	sob	run	skinny	cold
ocean	cry	thin	jog	sea	mug

4 Replace the words in brackets ( ) with a <u>synonym</u> (a word with the same meaning).

a The bus was coming down the (street) ______________.

b (Toss) ______________ the ball to me.

c Tessa put her cat's dinner into the (bowl) ______________.

d The princess wore a (lovely) ______________ dress.

e The (pupils) ______________ in my grade work very hard.

f Grandpa gave Rachel a (gift) ______________ for Christmas.

5 Use another word instead of *said* in the sentences below.

"How did you do that, Daniel?" ______________ Marcus.

Mum ______________, "Hurry up and go to bed!"

Your turn to write

Write a sentence or two about a time when you did something special. Circle any words where you could use a different word that means the same, and write that word above. Which word do you like best? Why?

Antonyms

An **antonym** is a word that means the opposite.

big – little

hot – cold

Dinosaurs

Dinosaurs lived a long time ago. ← Introduction to the topic

← Series of descriptions

Size

Some dinosaurs were much bigger than adult humans, but some were only little.

What dinosaurs ate

There were dinosaurs that ate meat and others that ate plants.

When dinosaurs lived

When dinosaurs lived it was sometimes hot and sometimes cold.

I wonder where they've gone now! ← End comment

1 Match each word with a word that means the opposite.

up	cold
hot	short
new	down
tall	no
boy	old
yes	girl

2 Finish this sentence. Use words from the list above.

A kettle is ____________ but a fridge is ____________ .

To the teacher

Play Simon Says using antonyms. For example: shut/open your eyes; stand up/sit down; stretch tall/be short; make a round/square shape; be quiet/noisy; look happy/sad. Then make a list of the opposites.

An information report is a series of descriptions about a topic.

Unit 24

These are antonyms: night  day  fat  thin 

3 Draw the pictures to show how each pair are opposites.

A **black** cat	A **white** cat
A **full** cup	An **empty** cup
A bird flying **high**	A bird down **low**
Something **slow**	Something **fast**

4 Write a sentence for each of these words to show they are opposites.

yummy ____

yucky ____

Your turn to write

Draw a picture of two animals that are opposite in some way. It might be an elephant and a mouse, a cow and a chicken, a snail and a lion . . . Then write a sentence for each animal to describe how they are different.

Connectives

Connectives link one sentence with the next.

First

Then

Next

After that

Finally

What I did this morning!

First I got up. → Then I got dressed.

Next I had my breakfast.

After that I cleaned my teeth.

Finally I walked to school.

Here I am at school!

Beginning
Who? What?

Sequence of events
things that happened in order

1 **Write words that make sense in this lifecycle of a butterfly.**

__________ an egg is laid on a leaf.

__________ a caterpillar hatches out.

__________ the caterpillar spins a cocoon.

__________ a butterfly is born.

Word bank

Next
Finally
First
Then

To the teacher

Discuss the morning routine that takes place in the classroom. Write the sequence on a chart or board using connectives as a model **before** the children attempt this activity. Explain the role of connectives in linking the sentences.

These are connectives: first → then → next → after that → finally

2 Write how you get ready for bed. Use the pictures to help you.

First I ____.

Then I ____.

Next I ____.

Finally I ____.

3 Now draw yourself asleep in your bed.

4 Who came first, next and last in this race?

First ________________ crossed the line.

Next ________________ crossed the line.

Finally ________________ crossed the line.

Your turn to write

How do you make a chocolate milk drink? Write down the steps it takes to make it. Use the words first, then, next and finally to begin your sentences.

Compound words are two words that are joined to make one.

seatbelt

airbag

What happened when Mum sneezed?

One day a little boy was sitting in the front seat. He was not wearing his seatbelt. ← **Orientation** When? Who? Where?

His mum sneezed! ← **Problem**

She slammed on the brakes! ← **Sequence of events** What happened?

The little boy went flying towards the front of the car, but the airbag saved him!

Now he always wears his seatbelt. ← **Problem solved**

by Ryan

1 Join two small words to make one bigger word. The first one has been done for you.

in + to = **into**

sun + shine = ______________________

back + bone = ______________________

2 Find a compound word from the Word bank to match these clues.

a The room you sleep in ______________________

b Saturday and Sunday ______________________

c A ball you kick ______________________

d Not inside ______________________

e A comfy place to sit ______________________

f You eat it ______________________

Word bank

 outside

 blackberry

 bedroom

 armchair

 football

 weekend

To the teacher

Make up some cards so the children can match two cards to make new compound words – give a picture clue to help. Encourage them to identify compound words as they read books too. They will thoroughly enjoy it!

A narrative is an entertaining story that relates a series of events that pose a problem and a solution played out by characters in a specific setting.

These are compound words:

seat + belt
seatbelt

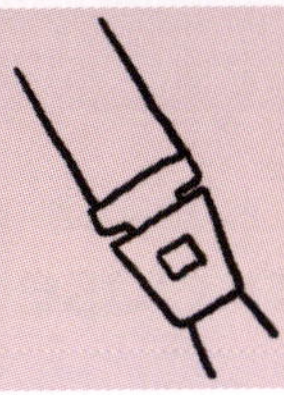

air + bag
airbag

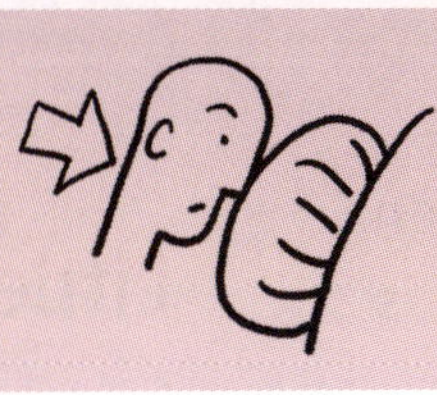

3 **Make some new compound words by joining words – one from each box.**

lady	room
bath	coat
tea	one
rain	bird
hand	not
every	bag
can	mother
grand	spoon

4 **Write your new words here.**

ladybird ______________ ______________

______________ ______________

______________ ______________

______________ ______________

5 **Fill the gaps with a compound word.**

a Sara saw a ______________ sitting on a leaf.

b I clean my teeth in the ______________.

c Pedro put on his ______________ when he went outside.

6 **Write a sentence of your own using compound words.**

____

____

Your turn to write

Draw a big picture of a handbag that your grandmother might like. Cut it out. Draw all sorts of things (which are compound words) that she may have in it, starting with **lipstick** and **toothpaste**. Share ideas with your friends.

Talking marks

Talking marks show when someone is speaking.

"Woof!"

"Moo!"

"Baa!"

"Coo!"

Little piggy-wig

Little piggy-wig on the farm close by,
All by himself ran away from the sty.
The dog said, "Woof!"
The cow said, "Moo!"
The sheep said, "Baa!"
The dove said, "Coo!"
Little piggy-wig began to cry,
And as fast as he could he ran back to the sty.

Anonymous

← **Title**

← **Rhyming words**
by
sty
cry

← **Short lines**

← **We don't know who the poet is**

1 Look at the poem. Put in the missing talking marks below.

a The dog said, Woof!

b The cow said, Moo!

c The sheep said, Baa!

d The dove said, Coo!

2 Now put talking marks before and after what is said.

a My teacher said, Do you need help?

b Corey said, It's lunchtime soon.

c Hurry up! Mum said.

d Curtis said, I'm going to ride my bike.

e Look at that big lizard! said Sophie.

f Little piggy-wig said, I'm running back to my sty!

To the teacher

Many books the children hear or read for themselves have conversation requiring talking marks. Read a story to the children, but before you start ask them to remember something a character says in the book. Afterwards write the conversation they remember on the board and model the correct use of talking marks.

Poems vary in structure but often have short lines and rhyming words.

Unit 27

These are talking marks: "Woof!" "Moo!" "Baa!" "Coo!"

3 This is a noisy farm. Write what each person or animal says. Remember the talking marks! The first one has been done for you.

The snail said, **"Hello!"**

a The horse said, ____________________

b The farmer said, ____________________

c The sheep said, ____________________

d The rooster said, ____________________

e The lady said, ____________________

f The cow said, ____________________

g The boy said, ____________________

4 Write something you might say to your:

Friend ____________________

Mum/Dad ____________________

Your turn to write

Draw a picture of your favourite farm animal. Write a short poem about it. See if you can make it rhyme!

Conjunctions

Conjunctions are words that join ideas.

1 Fill the gaps with so, and, because or but.

a Jess took her umbrella ______________ it looked like rain.

b We went to the shops ______________ they weren't open.

c Tom and Jo went for a bike ride ______________ had a swim in the river, too.

d I was hungry ______________ I made some toast.

Synonyms

Synonyms are words that have similar meaning.

2 Write a word from the Word bank below that means:

a tiny ______________

b cool ______________

c frightened ______________

d run ______________

e peep ______________

f smash ______________

g happy ______________

h lie ______________

Word bank

cold fib crash scared small glad look jog

Antonyms

Antonyms are words that have opposite meanings.

3 Write the opposite of the word in brackets.

a (boy) That ______________ is very tall.

b (quickly) The boat went ______________ down the river.

c (no) I asked Mum for a cake and she said, "______________."

d (clean) The car needed a wash because it was ______________.

e (night) Jeremy played all ______________.

f (sad) At the party Sara felt very ______________.

Connectives

Connectives link one sentence with the next.

4 Choose the best words from the Word box to start these sentences.

How to make a cheese sandwich

__________, butter two slices of bread.

__________, cut two pieces of cheese and put them on top of the butter. __________, put the other slice of bread on top.

__________, cut it in half and eat it!

Word box

Next
Finally
Then
First

Compound words

Compound words are two smaller words that join to make one bigger word.

5 Join two words together to make one.

a basket + ball = __________

b tooth + brush = __________

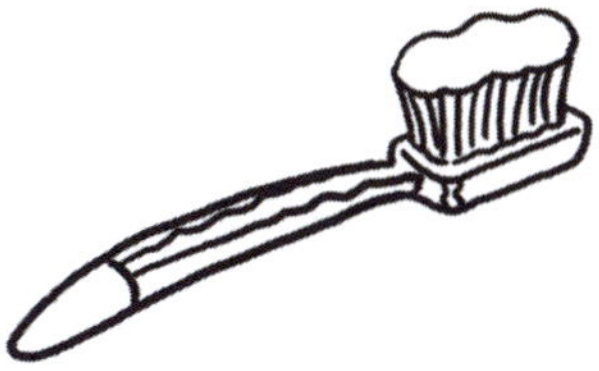

c eye + lash = __________

d in + side = __________

e water + melon = __________

f for + ever = __________

Talking marks

Talking marks are used to show when someone is talking.

6 Read this story and put in the missing talking marks.

"Oh dear," said Mother Bear.
Someone has been in our house," said Father Bear.
Look at the table! said Baby Bear.
Someone's been eating my porridge," said Father Bear.
"Someone's been eating my porridge, said Mother Bear.
Someone's been eating my porridge, said Baby Bear.
"And they've eaten it all up!

Alliteration is when lots of words begin with the same letter.

white

when

wind

walk

where

Clouds

← Title

White sheep, white sheep
On a blue hill,
When the wind stops
You all stand still.
When the wind blows
You walk away slow.
White sheep, white sheep,
Where do you go?

← **Rhyming words**
hill
still

← **Short lines**

by Christina G. Rossetti

← **Poet**

When we read 'When the wind blows/ You walk away slow.' we hear the 'w' sound lots of times. Alliteration is when the same sound is in lots of words that are together. It sometimes makes a tongue twister!

1 Fill in the missing words from the poem. They all have a w.

White sheep, **w**__________ sheep

On a blue hill.

W__________ the wind stops

You all stand still.

When the **w**__________ blows

You **w**__________ away slow.

W__________ sheep, white sheep,

W__________ do you go?

Draw a picture about this poem.

2 Circle the words that have the same beginning sound as in this poem.

washing eyes hair went car wing sheep window nest phone with

To the teacher

This poem describes the clouds as 'white sheep' on a 'blue hill'. They stop when the 'wind stops' and 'walk away' when the 'wind blows'. Discuss how the poet uses the image of sheep and the blue hill to describe the clouds.

Alliteration

Alliteration is when lots of words begin with the same letter

3 Each of these silly sentences has alliteration. Match the endings with the beginnings.

Beginning	Ending
Funny Fred fries	catch the clever caterpillar? 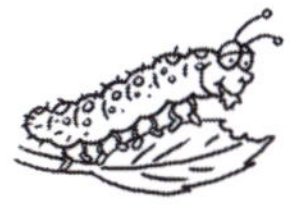
Can the crazy cockatoo	"Boom! Boom!" on his drum. 
"Mmm," mumbled Monty Mouse	licking lollies at eleven. 
Big Bad Ben banged	footy franks on Fridays. 
Lovely little Ellie likes	"My mum makes yummy mushies!" 

4 Circle the letters that are the same in each sentence.

5 Complete these sentences using alliteration.
Use the Word bank to help you.

a Seven shiny sharks ______________________________

b Googly goggles ______________________________

c Crazy cars ______________________________

Word bank

crash	shivered	glitter	shook	cliff	glow	shone	gleam
swam	cupboard	shining	climb	sea	glass	crawl	gaze

Your turn to write

Write your own nonsense poem using some words that begin with the same sound.

Onomatopaeia

Onomatopaeia is when words sound like what they mean.

"Bubble," said the kettle

← Title

"Bubble," said the kettle,
"Bubble," said the pot.
"Bubble, bubble, bubble,
We are getting very hot!"

← Verses

← Words that rhyme
pot
hot

Shall I take you off the fire?
"No, you need not trouble.
This is just the way we talk –
Bubble, bubble, bubble!"

← Short lines

"Bubble, bubble, bubble" sounds like the noise the water makes when it's boiling.
"Crash!" sounds like the noise it makes when something crashes.

1 **What else might go "Bubble, bubble, bubble"? Draw a picture and write the word for something else that bubbles.**

soup

To the teacher

Teach the children this rhyme off by heart. When they say "Bubble, bubble, bubble," ask them to visualise the pot bubbling and say the words the way the bubbling pot sounds.

Onomatopaeia

Onomatopaeia is when words sound like what they mean.

2 Circle the words that sound like what they mean in this poem.

The weather is full of sounds …

Listen to the rain …
It tinkles
and sprinkles
and splishes and splashes.

Listen to the wind …
It bustles
and rustles
and hums and strums.

Listen to the hail …
It bangs
and twangs
and clatters and patters.

Listen to the thunder …
It rumbles
and grumbles
and bashes and crashes.

Listen to the weather
Listen to the sounds
You can hear them now
RUSTLE, rustle, rustle
SWISH, swish, swishshshshshsh …

3 Draw what these words make you think of!

Broom! Broom!	Crash!

Your turn to write

Think about the word *Crunch*. Make up a short poem about something you might crunch. (Rhyming words could be lunch, munch, hunch, bunch …)

Self-assessment

Self-assessment at this level usually means the teacher is working collaboratively with the student.

Recount: A recount retells what happened in a sequential order.

Tick ✓

Purpose: Does it tell what happened? ☐

Structure: When I write a recount, I include:

- an orientation telling who, where, when ☐
- events in order ☐
- a personal comment. ☐

Tick ✓

Grammar: I have used:

- nouns, e.g. shop, car, school ☐
- proper nouns, e.g. Tom, Sydney ☐
- pronouns, e.g. she, we, I ☐
- verbs about the past, e.g. ran, ate ☐
- time and sequence words, e.g. first, next ☐
- capital letters and full stops. ☐

Information report: An information report gives facts about things.

Tick ✓

Purpose: Does it give true information about things? ☐

Structure: When I write an information report, I include:

- a general statement ☐
- a series of facts. ☐

Tick ✓

Grammar: I have used:

- nouns, e.g. cat, fur, claws ☐
- present-tense verbs, e.g. swims, runs ☐
- adverbs (how) about the action, e.g. quickly ☐
- adjectives, e.g. fat, soft, sharp ☐
- pronouns, e.g. they, it ☐
- capital letters and full stops. ☐

Procedure: A procedure tells how to make or do something.

Tick ✓

Purpose: Does it tell how to make or do something? ☐

Structure: When I write a procedure, I include:

- a goal ☐
- the materials ☐
- the steps. ☐

Tick ✓

Grammar: I have used:

- verbs happening now e.g. mix, stir ☐
- adverbs, e.g. slowly, happily ☐
- prepositions, e.g. in, on. ☐

Self–assessment and reflection:

Types of writing I enjoy:	**I need to practise:**

Self-assessment

Self-assessment at this level usually means the teacher is working collaboratively with the student.

Narrative: A narrative tells a story with a beginning, a middle and an end with a problem solved.

Tick ✓

Purpose: Does it tell a story? ☐

Structure: When I write a narrative, I include:

- a beginning ☐
- a middle with a problem ☐
- an end with the problem solved. ☐

Tick ✓

Grammar: I have used:

- proper nouns, e.g. Sydney, Ann ☐
- common nouns, e.g. mouse, boy ☐
- pronouns, e.g. he, they ☐
- adjectives, e.g. furry, little ☐
- verbs, e.g. ran, ate ☐
- conjunctions to make bigger sentences, e.g. and, so ☐
- time and sequence words, e.g. once, then ☐
- talking (quotation) marks " ". ☐

Exposition: An exposition consists of arguments from one or more points of view.

Tick ✓

Purpose: Does the text give your opinion? ☐

Structure: When I write my opinion, I include:

- my point of view ☐
- my reasons ☐
- my ending comment. ☐

Tick ✓

Grammar: I have used:

- nouns, e.g. environment, boat ☐
- pronouns, e.g. I, you ☐
- verbs, e.g. love, think ☐
- time words to link my reasons, e.g. then, after ☐
- exclamation marks ! ☐

Explanations: Explanations explain how and why things happen.

Tick ✓

Purpose: Does it explain how or why something has happened? ☐

Structure: When I write an explanation, I include:

- what is being explained ☐
- details about how ☐
- an end statement. ☐

Tick ✓

Grammar: I have used:

- nouns, e.g. dog, cage ☐
- action verbs, e.g. wag, scratch ☐
- conjunctions, e.g. because, when ☐
- capital letters and full stops ☐
- questions marks ? ☐
- prepositions, e.g. in, under. ☐

Self–assessment and reflection:

Grammar I use correctly:	**What I know about my writing:**

Cross-Reference Chart

Key
Unit number–**Page number**

Focus	Book 1	Book 2	Book 3	Book 4	Book 5	Book 6
Nouns – common	1–**6**, 2–**8**	1–**6**, 2–**8**	1–**6**	1–**6**	1–**6**, 4–**12**	1–**6**
Nouns – proper	4–**12**, 5–**14**	4–**12**, 5–**14**	2–**8**	2–**8**	2–**8**	2–**8**
Nouns – collective				4–**12**	3–**10**	4–**12**
Nouns – technical						3–**10**
Nouns – plurals	6–**16**	6–**16**	3–**10**, 13–**30**	3–**10**	6–**16**	5–**14**
Pronouns	10–**24**	10–**24**	14–**32**	5–**14**, 6–**16**	5–**14**	6–**16**
Adjectives	8–**20**, 9–**22**	8–**20**, 9–**22**	4–**12**, 5–**14**	7–**18**, 8–**20**	8–**20**, 9–**22**	8–**20**, 9–**22**
Verbs	11–**26**	11–**26**, 12–**28**	8–**20**, 9–**22**, 10–**24**	10–**24**, 11–**26**, 12–**28**	10–**24**, 11–**26**	10–**24**
Verb tense	12–**28**, 13–**30**				12–**28**	12–**28**
Adverbs	15–**34**	15–**34**	12–**28**	13–**30**, 14–**32**	15–**34**	13–**30**
Prepositions	16–**36**	16–**36**	16–**36**	23–**50**	16–**36**	15–**34**
Phrases		17–**38**		24–**52**	17–**38**	16–**36**
Conjunctions	22–**48**	25–**54**	15–**24**	22–**48**	18–**40**	17–**38**
Subject and predicate						18–**40**
Clauses				25–**54**	13–**30**	19–**42**
Simple sentences	17–**38**	18–**40**	11–**26**, 20–**44**		28–**60**	20–**44**
Compound sentences					28–**60**	20–**44**
Complex sentences					19–**42**	20–**44**
Statement		19–**42**			21–**46**, 29–**62**	23–**50**
Question	18–**40**	20–**44**	18–**40**	17–**38**	21–**46**, 29–**62**	23–**50**
Exclamation	19–**42**	21–**46**	19–**42**	18–**40**	21–**46**, 29–**62**	23–**50**
Command		13–**30**			29–**62**	11–**26**, 23–**50**
Full stops	3–**10**	3–**10**	6–**16**, 7–**18**		21–**46**	
Capital letters	3–**10**	3–**10**	6–**16**, 7–**18**			
Commas			21–**46**	16–**36**	22–**48**	
Apostrophe – of possession				19–**43**	23–**50**	24–**52**
Apostrophe – of contraction	20–**44**	28–**60**	17–**38**	19–**42**	24–**52**	25–**54**
Direct speech	27–**58**	27–**58**	22–**48**	20–**44**	25–**54**	26–**56**
Indirect speech						26–**56**
Paragraphs						22–**48**
Synonyms	23–**50**	23–**50**		30–**64**	27–**58**	28–**60**
Antonyms	24–**52**	24–**52**		29–**62**	27–**58**	28–**60**
Compound words	26–**56**	29–**62**				
Figurative language		30–**64**	29–**62**	27–**58**		29–**62**, 30–**64**
Alliteration	29–**62**	30–**64**	30–**64**	26–**56**		
Onomatopoeia	30–**64**	30–**64**		28–**60**		30–**64**
Metaphor						30–**64**
Review units	7–**18**, 14–**32**, 21–**46**, 28–**60**	7–**18**, 14–**32**, 22–**48**	23–**50**, 24–**52**, 25–**54**, 26–**56**, 27–**58**, 29–**62**	9–**15**, 15–**34**, 21–**46**	7–**18**, 14–**32**, 20–**44**, 26–**56**, 30–**64**	7–**18**, 14–**32**, 21–**46**, 27–**58**